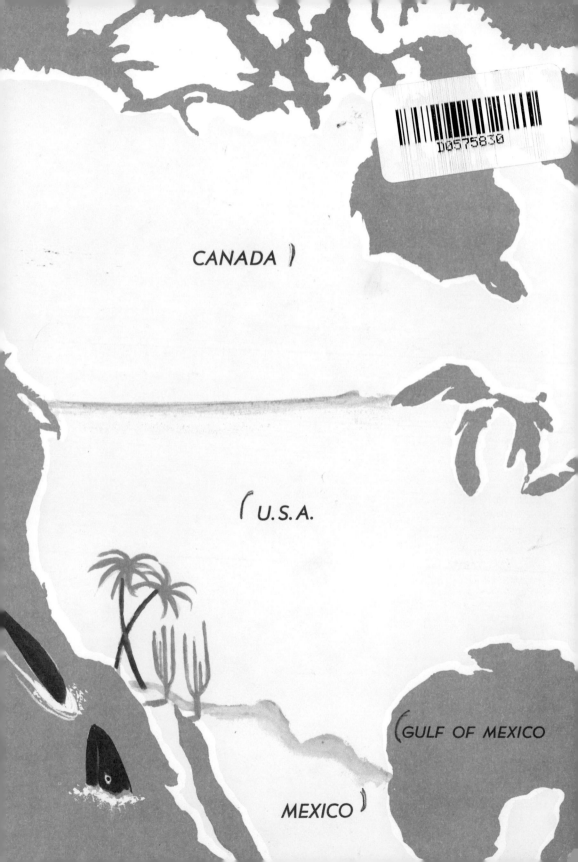

CANADA)

(U.S.A.

(GULF OF MEXICO

MEXICO)

THE WHALES GO BY

by

FRED PHLEGER

Illustrated by

PAUL GALDONE

Beginner Books

A DIVISION OF RANDOM HOUSE, INC.

This title was originally catalogued by the Library of Congress as follows: Phleger, Fred B. The whales go by. Illustrated by Paul Galdone. [New York] Beginner Books; distributed by Random House [1959] 62 p. illus. 24 cm. 1. Whales—Juvenile literature. I. Title. PZ10.P55Wh 59-9740 ISBN 0-394-80009-5   ISBN 0-394-90009-X (lib. bdg.)

I am big. I am a whale.

I am a gray whale. My home is here
in the cold ocean. Many other gray
whales live here in the cold ocean too.

I am big and fat. I do not see a thing
in all this ocean as big as I am.

A man is not as big as I am. These boats
are not as big as I am. Two boats are not as
big as I am. Three boats are not as big.
Four of these boats are about as big as I am.

I look like a fish. I swim in the ocean
just like a fish. But I am not a fish.
Like you, I breathe air.
My nose is up on top of my head.

When I go down in the water

I do not breathe for a long time.

When I come up again

I blow out the old air

and breathe in new air.

One day a big wind comes up.

The wind blows up big waves.

The big waves get water in my nose.

I do not like it.

It is too cold now in this ocean.

It is time for us to go away.

We must go to our winter home.

Our winter home is in the warm ocean.

We are on our way!

Now I am with the other whales.

We swim south near the land.

We must look at the land by day

to see the way to go.

We can see it from a long way.

We are led by two old whales. They
know the way south to the warm ocean.
They have gone there many times.

From time to time I stop to eat.

The other whales stop to eat too.

I eat all that I can hold.

I eat all kinds of little things

that are in the water.

I have to eat many, many of them.

They are so little! And I am so big!

We have come a long way.

And we have a long way to go.

We are tired now. We go to sleep.

Just as you do. We are so tired.

We sleep when we are tired.

But we sleep on top of the water.

We sleep on top of the water

for we must breathe when we sleep.

On we go, day after day.
We swim and swim for many days.

We look at the land. Day after day
we see new things. There are big hills.
They are high. We can see trees
on them. The land is green. The tops
of the hills are white. We know
where we are and where we must go.

One night the wind blows fast.
The waves on the ocean are big.
The night is black. I can not see
where I am. I can not see the
other whales. Bump! I hit something!
I can not see what it is.

A big wave hits me. Over and over
I go. I try to swim. I can not.
Another wave! It picks me up.
It dumps me. Plop!
Where am I . . . ?

I am on the sand.

I can not swim. I try and try.

There is too little water over the sand.

What will I do . . . ? I am

so tired! The night is so black!

Now at last the sun comes up.
It is day again. There is more water
here now. The water is high.
At last I can get away.

I am happy. I blow in and out.

The other whales are gone.

I must go after them.

We swim day and night, and night
and day. Now the ocean is not so cold.
But it is a long way yet
to our winter home.
What is that over there?

It is too big for a whale.

I do not have time to stop and look.

I swim on.

We do not stop to sleep.

We do not stop to eat.

We swim on and on.

Now there is something new!

The girl can go on top of the water.

I wish I could do that too.

But we can not stop yet.

We have to get to our winter home.

Now I swim by big trees. They are like the trees on land. But they are in the ocean. These are big ocean trees.

All kinds of fish make a home
in the ocean trees. There are red fish,
and green fish, and yellow fish.
These are warm water fish.

Now we see some seals.

The seals swim in the ocean.

But they can go up on land too.

Many, many seals have a home here.

Seals are like dogs. They are
the dogs of the ocean. Seals are fun
and we like them a lot.

We like the porpoises too. They jump
high out of the water. They splash!
Porpoises look like fish. But they are
not fish. They breathe air as I do.

Porpoises jump and play all the time.

They can swim fast. I wish

I could swim as fast as a porpoise.

But why do the porpoises go away?

I jump high to look. I see black

things in the water. Way over there!

I know what those black things are.

That is why the porpoises swim away.

These are whales that kill other whales.

They are called killer whales.

The killer whales kill porpoises too.

But they are after us.

Here they come. They come fast.

We swim as fast as we can.

We all try to get away.

But I can not swim

as fast as the killer whales.

I swim and swim and swim.
As fast as I can! The killer whale
is after me. The killer whale will
bite me. What can I do? I go
down deep in the water to get away.

When I come up the killer whales are
gone. They saw the porpoises. Now they are
after them. They are not after me now.
The porpoises jump high and fast. They get
away too. I must get away from here.

At last we can see the way into
our winter home. The way is not big.
We have to swim in line to get in. One
after the other. It is not deep. There are
waves. We can just make it. We have
come a long way. We are so happy!

And here we are in our winter home.

It is called a lagoon.

It is the lagoon of the gray whales.

The water is warm here.

We will be here a long time.

Here I will have my baby whale.

And this is my baby whale. She is
my new baby and I am her mother.

She is as long as two men
but she is little for a gray whale.
After all she is just a baby.

She has spots and a nose on the
top of her head just as I have.

She is at home in the water.
The water holds her up and
she can swim right away.

I show my baby whale how to swim
and breathe air at the same time.
We go to the top of the water.
Then I blow and she blows at the
same time. One big blow and one little
blow! Baby whale and I swim all over
the lagoon and blow at the same time.

One big blow and one little blow!
We look at the high hills of sand.
We look at all the things that fly
over us. We look at the many kinds
of fish that swim near us.

My baby whale takes milk from me
the way a baby cow takes milk. She
takes it as we swim next to one
another. She takes all she can hold.
She must get big as fast as she can.

One day, baby sees a boat.

It is a boat with men in it.

She wants to look at it, and swims near.

She jumps to the top of the water.
Splash! The men in the boat get
water all over them. They go away
from her fast. And she swims away fast
from them. It is funny to see how
fast they get away from one another.

There are many mothers and baby whales
in our lagoon. We have fun. Some of us
jump out of the water and fall.
Splash! We get water in our noses.
But we have fun.

The baby whales look at the big whales.

Some of the baby whales play too.

Just like the big whales. They jump.

They fall. They splash!

Now, too soon, it is the time of
year to go back. We must swim back
to our other home in the cold ocean.

It is a long way for the baby whales
to swim. It will take a long time.
Baby whales and mother whales
blow at the same time as they go.
One big blow and one little blow.
As far as you can see.

Many of us will come back again.

We will come back again next year.

We always have.

We always will.

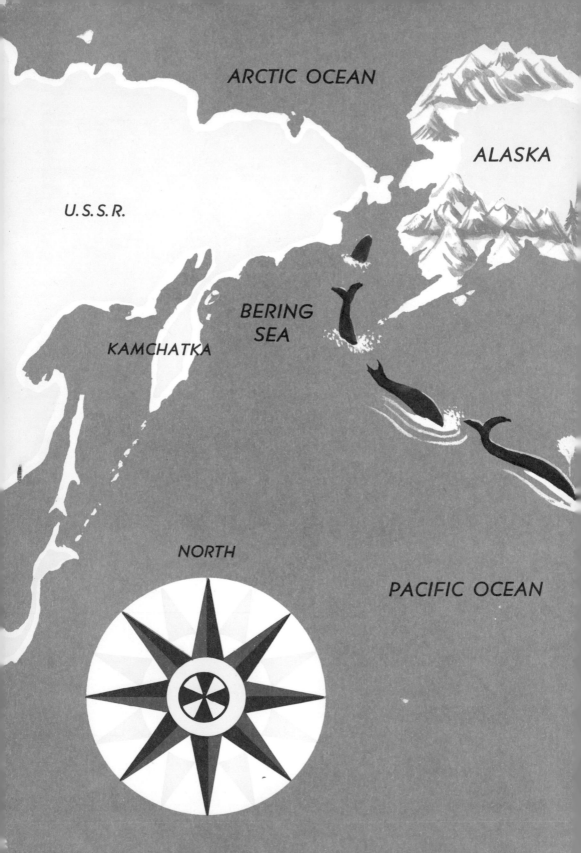